The LITTLE INSTRUCTION BOOK for babies

Kate Freeman

summersdale

THE LITTLE INSTRUCTION BOOK FOR BABIES

With research by Anna Martin

Illustrations by Kostiantyn Fedorov

Disclaimer
The advice in this book is purely for the purpose of entertainment and should not be followed.

Summersdale Publishers Ltd
46 West Street
Chichester
West Sussex
PO19 1RP
UK

www.summersdale.com

Printed and bound in the Czech Republic

ISBN: 978-1-84953-630-1

Substantial discounts on bulk quantities of Summersdale books are available to corporations, professional associations and other organisations. For details contact Nicky Douglas by telephone: +44 (0) 1243 756902, fax: +44 (0) 1243 786300 or email: nicky@summersdale.com.

To..

From..

Babies are always more trouble than you thought — and more wonderful.

Charles Osgood

Being a baby is a bewildering business – everything is new and there to be explored, and ultimately chewed or rubbed into the carpet. Who is going to hold your sticky hand and teach you the difference between a raisin and a rabbit poo, or help solve that perennial problem of where to wipe your nose when you haven't got a tissue? Because let's be honest, your parents don't know much – they don't even know what you want when you're crying!

Don't worry, though: help is at hand in the form of this little instruction book, which will guide you safely through the pitfalls and pleasures of those early years, and most importantly teach you how to get your own way. Enjoy!

Furiously squeeze your squeaky toy when you're in the library.

Eat ants and spiders.

Refuse to have your nose wiped – it's *your* snot and you might get hungry later.

You've done your first poo in the potty, how should you celebrate?

 Insist on applause for your achievement, and all subsequent achievements.

 Refuse to let your mum flush it away.

 Tip it up.

 Insist on eating dessert first and then having no room left for your main course.

Show your belly button to strangers.

What's the best way to stamp your creativity on your home?

 Colour in your parents' designer wallpaper – it'll make it unique.

 Blow your nose into your mum's favourite cushions.

 Make prints on the walls with your jam hands.

Insist on trying other people's drinks, and then dribble into them.

Stay up all night, just because you can.

Eat your bedtime storybook before your parents get a chance to read it to you.

Only use your parents' touch tablet with sticky fingers.

What should you do on breaking wind in polite company?

 Giggle, then point at the nearest adult.

 Say proudly: 'I'm just like Mummy now!'

 Follow through.

Have fun in Mum's make-up bag.

Try to ride the dog.

Demand that the TV is fixed on the cartoon channel during your waking hours. Throw a hissy fit if you don't get to watch the same programme at least three times in one day.

Throw your water bottle on the floor after each swig.

Develop a Velcro fixation and undo anyone's shoes that are fastened with it.

Wear your muddy wellies while climbing on your parents' bed.

Tear the covers off magazines and books.

Sneeze in people's faces when
they pucker up for a kiss.

Splash in the muddiest puddles on the days when your parents have forgotten to dress you appropriately.

Look behind the television when people walk off screen.

Create your own vocabulary that only you, and eventually your family, will understand and use.

Vomit down a visitor's top when they pick you up to give you a cuddle.

Master how to call the emergency services on all telephonic devices.

Jam your toys behind the door.

You've successfully negotiated the barrier to the kitchen. What should you do?

 Drink from the cat bowl.

 Empty the contents of the cupboards onto the kitchen floor.

 Start making dinner for everyone using cat biscuits and cereal.

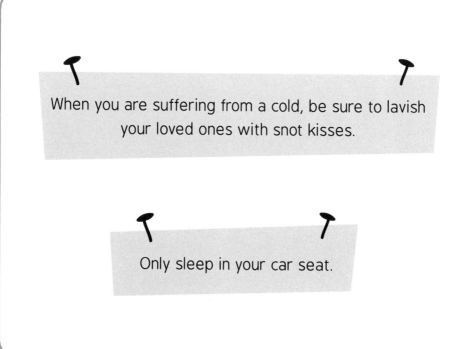

When you are suffering from a cold, be sure to lavish your loved ones with snot kisses.

Only sleep in your car seat.

Do your best to help at nappy-change time — lift those legs high. Score extra points for kicking your nappy changer in the face.

Always scream or laugh at cats — they love it!

Refuse to feed yourself with cutlery, but insist on feeding others with theirs.

 Screw up or draw on important documents.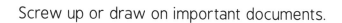

What should you do when you are dropped off at nursery for the first time?

 Stroll in without saying goodbye to your tearful parents and call your nursery teacher 'Mum'.

 Grab your parents' legs and not let go until they keel over.

 Waste no time in establishing your place by dealing in contraband rusks.

Be an angel with Grandma, but a devil for your mum.

Develop an obsession with watching the Grand Prix, and follow the cars across the TV screen with your sticky fingers.

Post credit cards and coins through gaps in the floor.

Post Mum's keys through the letterbox.

Always place raspberries on the ends
of your fingers before eating.

Make it your mission to prove that no nappy is leak-proof.

Glue your fingers together when making your first paper collage.

Who do you love best?

 Mummy and Daddy, because they do everything for me.

 Grandma and Grandpa, because they let me get away with everything.

 Whoever feeds me chocolate.

Lick or bite fruit or vegetables
at the supermarket, then
put them back.

Insist on saying a few words to whoever is on the phone, regardless of whether you know them.

Insist on taking naps on someone's knee, rendering them immobile for at least two hours.

Find your way into shop window displays and wave at passers-by.

Practise your best 'drunk man' impression while at the supermarket – walk in a wavy line and speak incoherently but with conviction.

Stick modelling clay in your hair.

Hurdle out of your cot if your parents don't arrive quickly enough when you call them.

Leave your slobber on pretty much everything.

Always find a way to reach things that are meant to be out of reach.

How should you behave on a play date?

 Insist that all toys belong to you – your friend should have brought toys with them if they wanted to play with something.

 Go to sleep in the Wendy house.

 Wipe your paint-covered hands on the curtains.

Always pull a face or stick your tongue out when someone points a camera at you.

Try walking while wearing your sleeping bag.

Tinker with your parents' alarm clock so they get up extra early – that way there's time for two breakfasts in the morning!

If your mum and dad say no, ask your grandparents.

Insist that you need to read whatever your parents are reading first, by grabbing the book / magazine /newspaper and not letting go.

It's family photo time — what should you do?

 Pull a face.

 Ruffle your parents' hair with sticky hands.

 Projectile vomit.

 Use your hairbrush to groom the cat.

Always lose one sock, or one shoe.

Cry at men with beards.

Believe people can't see you when you put your hands over your eyes.

Have a tantrum at the supermarket checkout.

Develop a squint or a limp, just to worry your parents.

What's the best course of action when your parents are in a hurry and need to get you fastened in the buggy?

 Make yourself as stiff and non-bendy as possible.

 Have a poo – make it a really messy one.

 Insist on taking several toys, which you need to find first.

Be terrified of Father Christmas and the Tooth Fairy.

Forget how to walk when you're having
your first proper pair of shoes fitted.

Always spill drinks, especially your own.

Eat any small morsels of food attached to the carpet – they taste better after they've had a few days to mature.

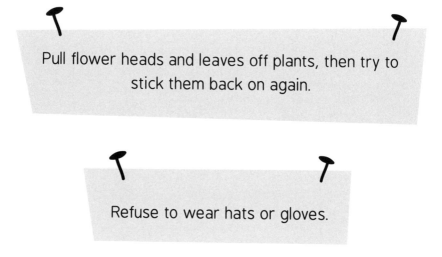

Pull flower heads and leaves off plants, then try to stick them back on again.

Refuse to wear hats or gloves.

If someone picks you up for a cuddle, either pinch their nose or stick your finger in their eye.

When eating peas, always eat one, then throw one.

Pull at loose threads on clothing and furniture and take delight in watching the thread grow and grow before your very eyes!

Put your potty on your head and shout 'Bum!'

Have a rummage in shopping bags and handbags.

Always scream at doctors.

Swear like Daddy.

What should you do when you receive a gift?

 Place it on the floor and walk over it a few times because it makes a nice crinkly noise.

 Rip the gift open with gusto, then throw the contents away and have hours of fun playing with the wrapping paper.

 Bite it, chew it, head-butt it, then throw it in the nearest bin.

Demand to listen to the same song over and over again at bedtime.

Cry at weddings, loudly.

Get your head stuck in the cat flap.

Once you've mastered the word 'no', insist on answering every question with it. Say it firmly and with authority – assert your independence early.

Hide under mummy's dress at social gatherings.

Learn how to make a bid
on eBay but make sure it's
for something useful, like an
industrial supply of marshmallows
or a combine harvester.

Stand on any toy with wheels and try to ride it.

 Insist your parents take you out for a drive at night to get you to sleep.

Say no when you really mean yes.

On a hot summer's day, when your grandparents are napping in their deckchairs, use the time wisely by cracking open the colour pens and carefully drawing along the lines on their legs.

Wipe your nose on your smart clothes.

Try on your mum's best shoes and attempt to walk in them.

Learn to rhyme words early on, especially ones that are rude.

Suck fabric labels on your cuddly toys.

Throw any unwanted food onto the floor, preferably pre-chewed or torn into tiny pieces.

Use the display toilet at the bath showroom.

Where should you wipe your nose when you haven't got a tissue?

 In a prominent place on your clothes.

 In a prominent place on someone else's clothes.

 On the cat.

Post jigsaw pieces down the back of your Babygro so whoever changes your nappy next gets a surprise!

 Finally nod off just as your parents are parking the car.

Pull the heads off dolls, especially someone else's.

Try putting any round, flat objects in the DVD player – rusks make particularly good television.

Dress the cat in one of your old Babygros.

Draw a picture of your mum
and give her a moustache.

Only show interest in
the noisiest toys.

What was your first word?

 Mama.

 Dada.

 Telly.

Make it your mission to climb onto every piece of furniture and base-jump off it.

Seek out the sharpest, most dangerous objects in the house and hand them to your mother when you have visitors.

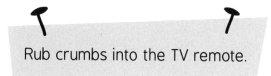

Learn how to undo buttons so you can cause maximum embarrassment when sitting on a visitor's lap.

Rub crumbs into the TV remote.

What's the best way to attract the waitress's attention at a restaurant?

 Flutter your eyelashes and giggle.

 Apply liberal amounts of lunch to your face.

 Use your fork as a catapult and fire olives at her.

How should you behave at the dentist?

 Clamp your jaws shut.

 Scream blue murder until you're issued with a lollipop.

 Strew the contents of the toy box around the waiting room.

Master the quivering bottom lip as early as possible – it's vital for getting your own way.

Water the carpet with your free-flow cup.

Never allow your cuddly toys to be washed.

Learn how to open doors from an early age – it's so much quicker than trying to get someone's attention and waiting for them to open doors for you.

Colour in your parents' newspaper.

Chatter constantly, but be rendered dumb when a phone is placed next to your mouth.

Make sure your parents get a good soaking when you're having a bath.

Learn how to roll for the
first time while you're having
your nappy changed.

What is your favourite toy?

 A sock with a hole in it.

Daddy's toolkit.

 Mummy's make-up bag.

Rock in your highchair and laugh as your parents turn white.

When's the best time to relieve yourself?

 When you're on the scales at the weigh-in.

 When your nappy has just been opened for changing.

 Just after the nappy change.

When you've had enough of walking, just stage a sit-down protest until someone picks you up and carries you to your desired destination.

Fall asleep face-down in your dinner.

Gravitate to the most expensive and breakable ornaments in other people's homes.

Where should you tidy your toys away at night?

 On the stairs.

 Jammed behind the door.

 In the cat basket.

Learn how to set the alarm on any type of phone, tablet or computer before you're two years old.

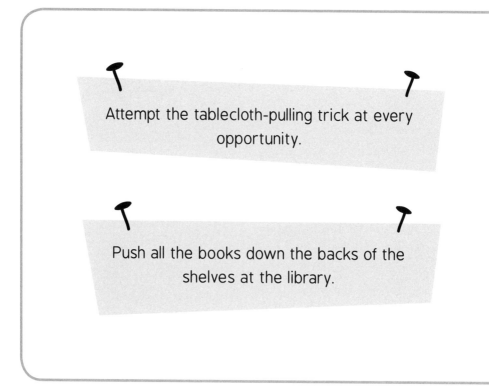

Attempt the tablecloth-pulling trick at every opportunity.

Push all the books down the backs of the shelves at the library.

Freak out your parents by putting both legs in one leg of your Babygro, so you look like a mermaid.

Poo at inopportune moments – like when you're being christened and everyone is watching.

If anyone should be foolish enough to put their finger in your mouth, bite hard.

If you're interested in finding out more about our books, find us on Facebook at Summersdale Publishers and follow us on Twitter at @Summersdale.

www.summersdale.com